MIKE PENCE BOOK

The Biography of Mike Pence

University Press

CONTENTS

INTRODUCTION

The day of the presidential election in 2016 looked gloomy for Vice-Presidential Candidate Mike Pence. Every major news outlet was certain Hillary Clinton would win the election and become the next president of the United States. As the day ticked by, political pundits and forecasting organizations became increasingly bold in their prediction that Donald Trump would lose.

As state after state declared for Hillary, Mike Pence's heart must have sunk. When the experts within Trump's campaign were expecting the loss, and when Trump himself reserved a small hotel ballroom in which he planned to give a concession speech, it seemed Mike's hopes of becoming Vice President—and perhaps President one day himself— seemed to shatter before him. He gathered with his family to view the polls, but all seemed lost.

Waiting for the axe to fall is not fun, but when that

axe takes an entire day and night to finally finish its devastating arc, one has time to think. If Mike Pence took time to reflect on the direction his life had been going up to this point, he certainly had a lot of personal and political history to keep him company.

He'd been a lawyer, once, the chosen profession of almost all politicians before they began their public career. He'd been a talk show host, as well, and he'd once been called "Rush Limbaugh on decaf," a high compliment that would win over Limbaugh fans and Limbaugh haters alike. He'd embraced conservativism and politics as a young man, diverging from the political sensibilities of his own family. He'd found a true calling in conservative politics and Christian values, a path he'd followed for almost all of his adult life.

Pence had served in the US House of Representatives, as well. He served on the Tea Party Caucus, and he managed to hold onto his title of Congressman for 12 years strong. And, while in the House, media experts pointed him out as a top choice for president on more than one occasion. But Pence stayed the course, following his own values and conscience. He remained steady instead of jumping ahead and committing political suicide by biting off more than he could chew. He crossed over from the legislative branch to the executive branch after that, becoming Governor of Indiana, and he pushed an aggressively conservative policy for his state with regard to taxes, gun control, and education, among other issues.

But the crowning moment—so far—of Mike Pence's political career had been when he won over two other shortlisted prospects and was asked to join Trump's ticket as the Vice-Presidential candidate in 2016. They'd come so far in this election, but now, as the sun set and Election Day drew to a close, there was little more they could do to change the course of their political careers. All that was left was to wait for the axe to fall and watch Hillary Clinton win.

But that's when the unthinkable happened.

A Last-Minute Reversal

Democratic elections are put on a high pedestal around the world, and for good reason. And yet this one convention, this representation of democratic ideals, can also get messy. Elections often twist and turn in mysterious ways, making them nearly impossible to reliably predict in many cases. Pence knew this all too well since he served in the House of Representatives and served on the House Select Committee to Investigate the Voting Irregularities of August 2, 2007.

Now, on the night of October 7, 2016, the tides were suddenly turning. Trump was doing surprisingly well in states he expected to lose. New reporters were just as shocked as the rest of the world as key states, like Florida, Iowa, and North Carolina, showed a Trump majority. It was a confusing and exciting time for the American people, and conservative voters, MAGA hats and all, were slowly realizing that they were not quite the minority they'd always thought of themselves as.

Still, as the night wore on, Hillary refused to concede. Outside sources say that members of Obama's staff called members of Hillary's campaign, warning her that it looked like she was not going to secure the win. Later, Obama himself reportedly spoke directly to Hillary on the phone, urging her to concede before it was too late, allowing the integrity of government to reign supreme.

By 2:30 the next morning, Wisconsin gave its ten electoral votes to Trump, giving him and Pence the 538 they needed to secure a win.

Over the course of a single evening, the tides had turned. Mike Pence would be the next Vice President of the United States!

The Start Of An Epic Battle

Trump threw a massive party at the New York HQ for his campaign. When Mike Pence got an opportunity to speak, he kept his victory speech short and sweet, surrounded by his family, wife, and adult children.

He spoke of the power of the voice of the

people, saying that America had selected its next "Champion."

That word—champion—was an interesting choice. While Mike Pence had gone through his own political and spiritual journey up to this point, securing the win to become Vice President would not be the end of his story. Instead, he would soon face an incredible and epic battle. He and President Trump would indeed have to be champions in the face of adversity.

The US would become embroiled in controversies and social upheaval. Trump's enemies would be loud and unyielding. And beyond that, COVID-19, the greatest national emergency this country has faced since the Civil War, would test Pence's fortitude in ways he could not imagine. Finally, as the term neared its end, Pence would find himself in an impossible position, having to act without and against his own president in the name of justice, democracy, and virtue.

In the pages that follow, we'll take a look at Mike Pence's life, starting with his childhood and schooling. We'll see his first steps into politics and his early, rocky campaigns. We'll see the lessons he learned that taught him about civic responsibility and righteousness. Then we'll take a closer look at the campaign, elections, and term Pence participated in as Vice President. Finally, we'll look at the great tests on his integrity he faced on January

6, 2021, as well as his activities after leaving office.

This book is about a man that has been quietly and stoically a great American hero, a man that thinks before leaping, and a man of virtue and patriotism, a man named Mike Pence.

CHAPTER 1

Early Life

B efore Mike Pence, there was his father, Edward. Edward Pence was an American hero, and he had the good fortune of being a hero when patriotism was high, and heroism was praised by almost everyone. In 1950, the Korean War broke out, a war that was yet another skirmish in the long string of bloody conflicts that grew out of the Cold War like toxic grape clusters along the same poisonous vine. Edward Pence, whose full name was Edward Joseph Pence, Jr, was sent to Korea as part of the US Army on the same year that "the American soldier" was named Man of the Year by Time Magazine.

Edward was of German and Irish descent, and his father, Edward Joseph Pence, Sr, worked long days in the stink and filth of the Chicago Stockyards, the epicenter of the American meatpacking industry in the middle of the 20th century, an empire that would gain Chicago the nickname "the hog butcher of the world." Edward Jr loved the Chicago area, but he dreamed of making something of himself, of starting his own company and not working in "the yards."

By 1953, the Korean War had died down to a stalemate, an armistice, and the establishment of the Korean Demilitarized Zone. Overall, about 3 million people died in the war—most of whom were civilians—but Edward made it home to Chicago as the proud recipient of the Bronze Star, a military decoration awarded to soldiers for heroic achievement or service. (Mike Pence, Edward's son, would go on to display his father's Bronze Star in his congressional, gubernatorial, and vice-presidential offices, proud of his father's heroics and values.) Happy to be home, young Edward set his sights on a new objective: starting a family.

He met and married a fellow Chicagoan, a lovely young woman named Ann Jane Cawley, although her friends called her Nancy. Nancy was also of Irish descent, a daughter of two Irish immigrants. Her father, Richard Michael Cawley, drove a bus in Chicago.

Edward and Nancy settled in Columbus, Indiana, a small town far south of the booming metropolis of Chicago, just along the highway between Indianapolis to the north and Louisville and the

Indiana-Kentucky state line to the south. There, in Columbus, they had six children, one of whom they named Michael Richard Pence (named after Nancy's father, Richard Michael), Mike for short.

And so, in the year 1959, Mike Pence was born into a family of hard work and patriotic heroism, faith and tradition, and, of course, love. This was the heritage that would come to shape Mike's personality, values, and career, as we'll see in this chapter and the chapters that follow.

Growing Up Catholic In Columbus

To say that Columbus, Indiana is a small town would be an understatement. In the 2020 census, there were only a little more than 50,000 residents in this quaint rural town. Back in the mid-and-late-1800s, however, it was one of the largest communities in Indiana, which was mostly thanks to the railroad established there in 1844—the first railroad in the entire state. The difference between Columbus and other communities in the area, like Chicago and Indianapolis, is that it remained quaint over the years while the latter two actively sought urban growth and industry.

So, the Columbus Mike Pence grew up in was small, cozy, and stunningly beautiful. Much of that beauty comes from the collection of Modern architecture that fills the town and has done so since the mid-20th century. More recently, Columbus has been prominent in various lists of the best places to live or visit. For example, it was named one of "The Ten Most Playful Towns" by Nick Jr. Family Magazine in 2004, and National Geographic Traveler ranked it 11th on its list of historic destinations that one should make plans to visit.

As a child, Mike loved stories of heroics and history. He inherited a love of traditional values and faith from his Catholic mother. In fact, Mike grew up in both a Roman Catholic and Democrat home. He even served as an alter boy, and if you were to ask a teen Mike Pence in the early 70s what political leaning he had, he'd definitely tell you he would be a lifelong Democrat.

He graduated from Columbus North High School in 1977, a school that had just changed its name a couple of years earlier after Columbus East High School was built in 1973. Mike's high school yearbook photo shows a young man with a tall face, a crooked grin, an amply mop of Irish curls, and the stern, flat eyebrows Pence would be known for decades later. While Mike's family certainly wasn't rich, his father, Edward, had done well with his dream of owning his own business. At this point, he was the owner of a small chain of gas stations, making enough money to send his son to Hanover College, a Presbyterian private college in nearby Hanover, Indiana.

College And Conversion

Two big changes happened for Mike while he attended Hanover College: he became a protestant, and he became a Republican.

Hanover College is the oldest private college in the State of Indiana. It was founded by Reverend John Finley Crowe in 1827, and although it is affiliated with the Presbyterian Church, it certainly does not require all its alumni to subscribe to that particular flavor of Christianity. Mike, a Catholic, felt at home there. Over time, however, his religious views started to shift, and he became an evangelical, born-again Christian, much to the dismay of his mother back home.

As he entered college, Mike had two main interests: history and politics. He was already an active political volunteer, having worked for the Bartholomew County Democratic Party while he was still in high school. He'd been moved to become politically and socially active by men such as John F. Kennedy (who'd also been the only Catholic US President) and Martin Luther King Jr. In fact, it may not be surprising that Mike voted for Jimmy Carter —a Democrat—in 1980. It was the candidate that defeated Carter in that election that would later plant Republican seeds in Mike's mind, however.

Mike would later say that it was the "commonsense conservatism of Ronald Reagan" that would sway him into embracing the Republican Party. Mike was raised in a no-nonsense, traditional household, so he was certainly well-suited for conservative politics. Much later in life, Mike would still describe himself as a "principled conservative," saying, "I'm a Christian, a conservative, and a Republican, in that order." He'd also go on to be a supporter of the Tea Party Movement, a fiscally conservative movement that calls for lower taxes and reduced government spending.

So, going to college was certainly a transformational experience for Mike. He went into Hanover College, a Catholic Democrat, and left a Born-Again Republican. But his passion for political action, encouraged by heroes like JFK and Martin Luther King Jr, never wavered.

From Hanover To Law School

Mike, a lifelong lover of history, chose history as his major at Hanover. He graduated with a Bachelor of Arts in 1981. During his time at Hanover College, Mike had also become the chapter president of the Phi Gamma Delta fraternity, an organization established in 1848 and boasting well over 100 chapters across the US and Canada. From 1981 to 1983, he got work at Hanover as an admissions counselor. Then, in 1983, he moved to Indianapolis to study for a degree in law.

Indiana University-Purdue University Indianapolis, usually called IUPUI for short, is a public research university, the result of a partnership between Indiana University (which is a system of public universities across Indiana) and Purdue University (which is a university system that boasts a least one extension center in each of Indiana's 92 counties). The urban campus is in downtown Indianapolis along the White River and Fall Creek.

It was at IUPUI that Mike earned a Juris Doctor from the Indiana University's Robert H. McKinney School of Law, a school that distinguishes itself for excellence. In fact, several other distinguished leaders in politics attended the same school, including numerous senators, representatives, governors, and one other United States Vice President—Dan Quayle, who served under George H. W. Bush from 1989 to 1993.

After graduating from law school in 1986, Mike had his heart set on starting his own career in politics, although, as we'll see in the following chapter, that career got off to a rocky start.

CHAPTER 2

Campaigns and Radio

After Mike Graduated from law school in 1986, he started working as an attorney in a private practice, but his sights were already set on pursuing public life. He just needed to prepare for the right election to run in. Unfortunately, his first attempts at politics didn't turn out so well. As we'll see in the following section, Mike would lose two campaigns in a row. And yet, these experiences were essential for him to cultivate the strength of character that would define him later in his career.

Two Failed Congressional Races

The 2nd Congressional District in Indiana makes up the territory in the northern part of the state. This is where Pence ran against Philip Sharp in 1988 and again in 1990. This district has largely been

Republican for much of its history. For example, when it comes to presidential races, the district voted for George W. Bush in 2000 and 2004, the later election with Bush holding a solid 56% of the vote. In 2012, voters in the district voted for Mitt Romney, and they also voted for Trump with a stunning 59% in both 2016 and 2020. The only occasion Indiana's 2nd District has voted for a Democrat was with Barack Obama in 2008, and that was only by a 0.3% lead over John McCain.

As for congressmen, the district also had a strong record of electing Republican leaders. From 1935 to 1975, the district always had a Republican congressman. That changed with Floyd Fithian in 1975, however. Fithian is considered one of the "Watergate Babies," an expression given to politicians who won the vote in the wake of the infamous Watergate scandal that stretched from 1972 to 1974. The previous Representative, Earl Landgrebe, had been a staunch supporter of Richard Nixon. When Nixon lost almost all of the favor of the American public, many politicians that supported him also fell out of favor. Many were even suspected of being corrupt, guilty by association, as it were.

So, starting in 1975, this strongly Republican district started electing Democrat congressmen. First, Floyd Fithian, and then Philip Sharp after him, who was first elected in 1983.

Mike looked at the situation in the area—a classically Republican population that grew distrustful of Republicans thanks to Nixon—and figured he'd have a good shot of turning things around, restoring the people's trust in conservative politics. In other words, on this small scale, Pence was set up to be a sort of conservative messiah.

Unfortunately, things did not turn out that way. Pence lost to Sharp in 1988. He continued with his law practice, biding his time. Then, in 1990, he tried again, this time quitting his job in order to focus full-time on the campaign. Once again, however, he was unsuccessful.

A year later, Pence wrote and published an essay entitled "Confession of a Negative Campaigner." It originally came out in the *Indiana Policy Review*. Pence genuinely apologized for running negative attack ads during his campaigns. He swore in the essay that he would no longer use insulting speech in his campaigns, and he would not say or do anything that belittles his opponents.

These lessons, no doubt, helped to build character. But they also were hard pills to swallow. Pence would not revolutionize the district as he'd hoped. Another Republican, David M. McIntosh, would do that in 1995 by defeating Sharp and becoming the first Republican Congressman to represent the district since Watergate.

Pence was out of luck when it came to politics—at least for now. In the meantime, he had another way to get his voice and views out there: the radio.

Mike Pence On The Radio

After losing the 1988 campaign, Pence was offered a regular spot on the radio station WRCR-FM, which broadcast out of Rushville, Indiana. The radio show, called *Washing Update with Mike Pence*, was only a half-hour long, once a week, but it gave Pence a chance to speak on political issues that were important to him.

Later, in 1992, after having lost his second race, Pence was hired to do a daily talk show on the same station, this one called *The Mike Pence Show*. He also hosted a weekly show on Saturdays that broadcast out of WNDE, Indianapolis, allowing Pence to reach even more listeners. His show was syndicated in 1995, allowing him to broaden his reach to even more people. It ran from 9:00 in the morning until noon every weekday, and as many as 18 Indiana stations rebroadcast the show.

Also, in 1995, Pence started a public affairs TV show, which was also called *The Mike Pence Show*. Pence referred to himself as "Rush Limbaugh on decaf." The idea was to talk about conservative topics, just like Limbaugh, but without the bombastic style Limbaugh was known for.

Pence ended his radio and TV shows in 1999 because he wanted to focus on the 2000 campaign for Congress. Unlike the two campaigns he'd lost a decade before, Pence would make a success of this campaign, finally securing a public office. This campaign, as well as his time in the House of Representatives, will be the focus of the following chapter.

CHAPTER 3

Congressman Pence

David McIntosh had broken the record of Democrat congressmen for the 2nd Congressional District of Indiana, restoring the voters' faith in conservative politics. He took on the role of Republican Messiah for the region, a role Pence had hoped to fill in 1988 and 1990.

During his time as a congressman, McIntosh, who was able to take the seat because Sharp decided to retire in 1995, fought to get rid of government regulations within the health and food industries. He was also a member of the House Oversight and Government Reform Committee.

In 1999, McIntosh decided to run for Governor of Indiana. In the 2000 election, he lost to Democrat Frank O'Bannon. Later, in 2012, McIntosh ran for Indiana's 5th Congressional District, but he again lost. It seems McIntosh wasn't able to become the

Republican Messiah he might have hoped to be, after all.

That said, McIntosh dropping out of the running for Congress opened the way for Pence to run once again. This time Pence would be successful, winning the vote and being sworn in as Congressman Pence on January 3, 2001.

First Term In Congress

Although Pence was a Republican, he famously described himself as "a Christian, a conservative, and a Republican, in that order." That meant that, at times, he did not play ball with Republican leadership, opting to follow his own conscience instead.

For example, in his first year in office, Pence opposed the No Child Left Behind Act, even though it was being pushed strongly by then-President George W. Bush. This act, which was eventually signed into law on January 8, 2002, made provisions for underprivileged students. It also set standards for student excellence, even though many of the details of these standards were left up to each state to set. The act faced harsh criticism from both sides of the political aisle, although it did get passed by both chambers of legislature. Later, in 2015, a bipartisan Congress gave the act an overhaul, turning it into the Every Student Succeeds Act, which leaves even more of the regulation in the hands of the states.

Also, in his first term, Pence also opposed Bush's Medicare prescription drug expansion plan, which was signed into law on December 8, 2003.

Following Congressional Elections

Pence had an easy time holding onto his position as Congressman for several terms. For example, while he only won the vote in 2000 by just over 50%, the remaining 50% split among the Democrat, Independent, and Libertarian candidates, he won by 63.79% in 2002. In 2004, he won by just over 67% and would continue to win by at least 60% every other time he ran for Congress in that district.

Every year, Pence was the only Republican candidate, winning 100% of the vote in each Primary Election, with the exception of 2006, when George Holland made a play for the Republican Congressional ticket. Pence beat him easily with 86% of the vote in the primaries.

A Republican On The Rise

Through the mid-2000s, as Pence served as Congressman, he also began to rise through the leadership structure of the Republican Party. For example, during his first term, he served on the Congressional Committees for Agriculture,

Judiciary, and Small Business. The following term, he started working on the Committee for International Relations. In his fourth term, he served on the Select Committee to Investigate the Voting Irregularities of August 2, 2007.

On August 2, a vote was called in the House regarding the 2008 appropriations bill. Among other things, this bill would explicitly deny federal benefits to illegal immigrants. As the vote neared its end, several Democrat members changed their vote, and it appeared that this was a ploy to sway the results of the final count. Republican members took issue with this and boycotted the change in votes. The following day, a committee was established to review what had happened and make recommendations on voting rule changes within the House.

All of this may seem like minutia, especially if you don't follow politics too closely. But these committees are an important part of how Congress functions. Voting rules are very important because they'll affect every decision made in the future. Pence served as the Ranking Member of the select committee, and they issued a report by September 30 of the same year.

In 2006, Pence made a play for the minority leader position, which would make him the leader of the Republican Party within the House. He lost that race, and John Boehner of Ohio took on the role instead. Later, Pence would be made the Republican Conference chairman, with the third-highest-ranking Republican leadership position within the House.

Despite this setback, by 2008, Pence was making waves as an established politician and leader among his peers in the House. For example, *Esquire* magazine put him on their list of the ten best members of Congress in 2008. They said his "unalloyed traditional conservatism has repeatedly pitted him against his party elders." In that same year—and again in 2012—he was mentioned as a promising candidate for president, but Pence didn't opt to run on either of those occasions.

In fact, in 2010, the Values Voter Summit, a yearly political conference in Washington DC that focuses on conservative politics and social issues, pegged Mike Pence as their top choice for president. This came from a straw poll they conducted.

However, Pence didn't jump at any of these opportunities to run for president. Instead, he stayed on with the House of Representatives, Serving in the prestigious Foreign Affairs and Judiciary Committees. Then, in 2011, Pence announced that he had another goal in mind—running for Governor of Indiana.

CHAPTER 4

Governor Pence

When Mitch Daniels became Governor of Indiana in 2005, the state had not had a Republican governor for over 15 years. Conservative citizens of Indiana were no doubt thrilled to have a candidate who had worked closely with George W. Bush as the Director of the Office of Management and Budget. In fact, in order to make every possible reference to his time under Bush, Mitch Daniels used the slogan "My Man Mitch," a term Bush had once used when talking about Daniels.

Daniels campaigned around in a white RV, which he used to travel to each of Indiana's counties multiple times. The RV was decorated with the signatures of Mitch's supporters, a vehicle he nicknamed "RV-1", a reference to Air Force One.

Mitch Daniels was incredibly popular as Governor

of Indiana, and he set the pace for the state to have at least two more Republican Governors after him. After running for two terms, Daniels decided to leave politics and has since served as president of Indiana's own Purdue University. His finishing out two terms meant the door was open for another leadership figure to step in. Pence saw this opportunity and jumped on it.

The 2012 Election

Pence announced his intention to run for Governor of Indiana in May of 2011, meaning he'd have several months to prepare for the campaign that wouldn't take place until 2012. He was able to take all the lessons he'd learned over several congressional races up to this point to plan and execute a successful campaign.

The main thrust of Pence's platform revolved around Mitch Daniels' popularity as Governor. He touted Daniels' successes and promised that he'd continue in those same footsteps and continue to reform both education and business.

Even though Daniel was indeed quite popular and was endorsing his fellow Republicans completely, this race was no cakewalk. Pence found himself in a heated and difficult campaign against Democrat John R. Gregg.

Gregg had served in the Indiana House of

Representatives, and he'd even been the Speaker of the House. Just like Pence, Gregg was a polished and experienced politician, although his experience had been solely at the state level.

In fact, the race between Gregg and Pence was the closest gubernatorial electing Indiana had seen in 50 years. This may have partially been because Pence refused to use negative political ads, as he'd previously done early in his career. On the other hand, not going negative allowed Pence to keep the moral high ground, something he'd always strived to do, in line with his personal beliefs about integrity and strength of character. It wouldn't be until his run with Trump that his streak of avoiding negative and attack ads would be broken, and that was a case that was out of Pence's control.

Pence won the vote with just under 50%, a little less than 3% more than Gregg. He was sworn in as the 50th governor of Indiana on January 14, 2013.

Some Key Policies

Pence certainly kept his promise in supporting and continuing many of the policies and initiatives his predecessor, Mitch Daniels, had started. For example, Indiana had enacted right-to-work legislation on Daniels' watch, and Pence quickly found himself defending the legislation from those that aimed to overturn it. At the same time, however, Pence also made great strides on some key policies that he set for himself.

Daniels had left the state with a budget reserve of about $2 billion. According to the Wall Street Journal, Pence "added to that reserve under his watch, though not before requiring state agencies, including public universities, to reduce funding in year which revenue fell below projections." When it comes to fiscal and economic goals, Pence stated early on in his campaign that he wanted to reduce income taxes by 10%. While he didn't achieve the full cut he'd hoped for, he did manage to reduce state taxes significantly.

When it comes to education, Pence increased education funding in several significant ways. For example, funding for preschools, voucher programs, and charter schools increased. Pence even testified before the state Senate Education Committee personally in order to convince fellow Republicans of the value of a $10 million preschool pilot program he was pushing for. The preschool program was initially defeated, but Pence was able to revive it later. At the time, Indiana was one of only ten states in the US that had no arrangement for helping poor children get into preschool.

As a "Christian first," Pence was very publicly in favor of school teaching creationism to students. But his view on the matter was well balanced. He proposed schools teach both evolution and creationism, presenting the ongoing controversy and debate and allowing students to choose for themselves what they wanted to believe.

Pence's gun policy was another key area he made big changes during his tenure as Governor. He signed a bill that allows firearms to be kept in teachers' vehicles in a school parking lot, the idea being to give teachers some hope of defending themselves in the case of a shooting or attack on the school. After a shooting in Chattanooga in 2015, Pence recruited a civilian organization, the National Rifle Association, to train the Indiana National Guard on concealed carry, the idea being that more responsible, trained adults with weapons in public, the more protection there would be in general.

Pence outlawed certain abortions in Indiana, as well. For example, an abortion would be denied if the reason given had to do with the race or gender of the baby. Also, a law passed during Pence's tenure required that fetuses and aborted babies be buried or cremated. At the time, Indiana was the only state in the Union that required such a thing, but the law certainly reflected a traditional and Christian perspective on the respect of life.

A Re-Election Campaign That Was Halted

In 2016, Pence had every intention of running for

Governor once again, and it was clear that he would likely be able to win by a better margin than the previous term's election.

He won the Republican primary unopposed on May 3, 2016. John R. Gregg was back for more and won the Democrat primary. However, just two months later, everything changed in Pence's life when he was offered the chance to run as Vice President with Donald Trump.

Pence's running mate for the gubernatorial election was Eric Holcomb, a man from Indianapolis and fellow Hanover College alumni. When Pence announced he'd drop out of the race, Holcomb dropped out as a candidate for Lieutenant Governor. It didn't take Holcomb long to figure out he had a good chance at the governorship. He entered the bidding and won the Republican nomination against three other contenders.

Holcomb was very behind in the race by the time he started campaigning in earnest. This didn't dissuade him, though, and he managed to snatch the victory from Gregg with 51.4% of the vote. Around the same time, the Trump-Pence ticket won Indiana electoral points with a strong 56% of the vote.

Life was going to be very different for Pence after this. In the following chapter, we'll look at his vice-presidential campaign. Then, in the chapter that follows, we'll look at his tenure as Vice President of the United States.

CHAPTER 5

Vice-Presidential Campaign

People knew for a long time that Donald Trump planned to run for president in 2016. For decades, Trump had been talking about running nearly every time an election appeared on the horizon. He made bids for the candidacy a few times, even jumping from one party to another through the years. But it was in 2013 that Trump started seriously researching the possibility of running in the 2016 election. Finally, in February 2015, he did not renew his television contract for The Apprentice, which had run across fifteen seasons since 2004. That raised serious suspicions that Trump would run for president.

On June 16, 2015, he formally announced his candidacy after coming down the golden escalator at Trump Tower and heading into a rally and speech. From the start, he talked about issues like illegal immigration, jobs leaving the United States, and the national debt. He also stated that he'd be self-funding his campaign instead of accepting any money from donors.

From the start, Trump was embroiled in controversy, with media pundits picking apart everything he said. Trump, in turn, seemed to feed off the drama, fueling it every chance he got. However, throughout the rest of 2015 and far into 2016, Trump was running alone. There was no mention of a potential vice president or running mate. Who would Trump choose to stand by his side in the final months of the campaign?

The Vice-Presidential Vetting Process

In May 2016, Trump was pegged as the presumptive nominee. Even then, he hadn't started seriously looking at a potential running mate. Meanwhile, his rivals, Ted Cruz of Texas and John Kasich, the Governor of Ohio, had already started the vetting process on their vice-president picks. Cruz had selected Carly Fiorina, the once-CEO of Hewlett-Packard. During this time of the Republican presidential primaries, Pence publicly endorsed Ted Cruz.

The vetting process for a vice-presidential candidate involves a thorough examination of any public records that relate to the person. This would include looking at their finances and the speeches they've given. Once the preliminary vetting is done, a "full vet" follows. The nominee has to submit their tax records for analysis, fill out a series of questionnaires, and even provide access to their medical records.

After both Cruz and Kasich dropped out of the running, leaving Trump as the de-facto Republican candidate, his campaign started looking at possibilities for vice president. Attorney Arthur B. Culvahouse, Jr led the vetting process for the Trump campaign. Trump was first given a list of sixteen names in May. Finally, in June, campaign officials started vetting six of those sixteen.

While all this was happening, Trump was coy when asked about a running mate. He said he'd narrowed the list down to five or six people in May. Then, he told the press in July that he was considering about ten people. Media outlets and newspapers started providing their "inside" lists of candidates, although there was very little overlap in the lists and the suspicion was they were either making it up, or someone was lying to them.

By early July, many media outlets agreed that Trump had narrowed it down to a shortlist of three people: Christ Christie, Newt Gingrich, and Mike Pence. On July 14, 2016, Trump asked Pence to be his running mate. He planned to officially announce this the following day, but he ended up announcing it on

Twitter and holding a press conference on July 16.

Of course, as we already mentioned, Pence could not appear on the ballot twice, according to state law, so in order to accept the offer to be the vice-presidential candidate, he had to bow out of the campaign to be re-elected as governor. With the selection process complete, how would Pence succeed as part of the Trump campaign?

Immediately after accepting the role as candidate of vice president, Pence was flooded with questions regarding how he felt about some of Trump's promises and policies. Thus began a delicate balance Pence had to engage in to support Trump but be more diplomatic about it. He boldly talked about the things he was "in sync" with Trump about, including immigration issues and the wall along the Mexican border. Meanwhile, his solid conservativism was noted by some. FiveThirtyEight said that Pence was the most conservative vice-presidential candidate in 40 years.

The Vice-Presidential Debate

In October, Pence had the vice-presidential debate against the Democratic vice-presidential nominee Tim Kaine. In order to prepare for the debate, Pence had Scott Walker, the Republican governor of Wisconsin, play the role of Kaine. Both Pence and Kaine prepared hard, knowing that even the slightest edge they could lend to the campaign could prove necessary. Kaine had the lawyer Robert Barnett stand in for Pence during their debate prep.

The debate was held on October 4 at Longwood University, which is in Farmville, Virginia, and boasts of being one of the oldest institutions of higher education in the United States. The moderator was Elaine Quijano of CBS, making her the first Asian American to moderate a national US debate. She was also the youngest journalist to moderate a debate since 1988 and the first digital network anchor to be selected as moderator.

The debate format was fairly simple: It would last 90 minutes, allowing time for nine topics, each with a ten-minute time limit. Each candidate would have two minutes to respond to the opening question, and then the remainder of the time would allow for a back-and-forth and a deeper discussion of the topic.

Pence, Kaine, and Quijano sat at a table, and the debate went live. Quijano asked questions about Donald Trump's personality, the nation's economy, Social Security, relations between race and the police, nuclear weapons, abortion, and finally, religious faith.

Pence turned the debate into a massive success, mostly because of his stoic mannerisms and calmer nature. An instant poll from CNN showed that 48% of viewers felt Pence had won the debate, and only 42% thought Kaine had won. One of the biggest reasons had to do with Kaine interrupting Pence repeatedly—more than 70 times by one official count! Because of this, Kaine was seen as a hothead, and Pence was perceived to have a cooler temperament. He was seen as more reasonable and a better prospective leader.

Scandal And Suspense

Much of Pence's responsibility during the campaign was to publicly support Trump's claims and policies. That's what a good running mate does, after all. That said, Pence held his own moral high ground, and that meant that, at times, he had to stand up for what was right, even if that meant he stood differently than Trump.

For example, with less than a month remaining in the campaign, Trump came under heat from some lewd comments he'd made several years before. When reporters asked Pence about it, he told reporters: "I do not condone his remarks and cannot defend them." And yet, he still made it clear that he stood by Trump. After the debate, Pence was criticized for not defending Trump's comments as well as he could have.

In fact, because of the scandal around these comments from Trump, it has been reported that Reince Priebus, the Republican National Committee chairman at the time, reached out to Trump and encouraged him to drop out of the race "for the good of the party" and that Pence had agreed to replace Trump on the top of the ticket.

However, on October 10, when Pence talked to reporters on CNN and was asked about whether he was considering leaving the ticket, Pence made his response absolutely clear, saying, "It is absolutely false to suggest that at any point in time we considered dropping off this ticket." He continues, "It is the greatest honor of my life to be on this ticket."

As we saw in the introduction to this book, the election came right up to the wire. While Trump had been in some scandalous news cycles, so had Hillary Clinton. Still, few honestly expected Trump to win, including many within the Trump-Pence campaign. And yet, even though Hillary did get the majority of votes overall, the campaign Pence had worked so hard on had managed to secure enough electoral votes to secure a win.

Mike Pence would become the 48th vice president of the United States.

CHAPTER 6

Vice President

I mmediately after winning the vote, Pence was appointed chairman of the transition between Obama and Trump. This gave Pence a great deal of influence in the administration for a number of reasons. First, he was in a position as mediator between Trump and Republicans in Congress, having to reassure conservatives about Trump's conservative policies and plan. He was also instrumental in determining Trump's cabinet.

On November 10, Vice President Joe Biden and Pence sat down in the White House to discuss the transition of power. Finally, on January 20, 2017, at noon, Pence was sworn in as vice president. Justice Clarence Thomas swore him in. Pence put his hand on Ronald Reagan's Bible. In fact, he had the bible opened to the same verse That "No-Nonsense" Reagan had laid his hand on when he took office—

Chronicles 7:14, which says, "If my people, which are called by my name, shall humble themselves, and pray, and seek my face, and turn from their wicked ways; then will I hear from heaven, and will forgive their sin, and will heal their land."

Pence immediately sprang into action as vice president. On the same day he was sworn in, he performed several ceremonial duties that got the new administration jump-started. For example, he swore in Jim Mattis as the Secretary of Defense, as well as John Kelly as secretary of Homeland Security. The White House senior staff are not sworn in in the same way that a cabinet member or elected official would be, but pence administer the oath of office to two members of the senior staff two days after taking office himself.

What would follow would turn out to be an intense series of victories and difficulties for the Trump-Pence administration. In this chapter, we'll look at the first three years of Pence's term and seeing some of the decisive actions pence took while in office prior to the COVID-19 pandemic.

Pressure On Iran

Ever since its war with Iraq, Iran has repeatedly performed missile tests in order to increase its military capabilities Two of those missile tests were conducted in 2017, at the very beginning of

Pence's term. After the tests conducted on January 29, the Trump administration imposed a number of sanctions against the country. Michael T. Flynn, Trump's National Security Advisor, said, "the days of turning a blind eye to Iran's hostile and belligerent actions toward the United States and the world community are over."

On February 5, Pence stepped up to defend the actions of his administration, warning Iran "not to test the resolve" of the US when it comes to testing ballistic missiles. One could certainly argue that Pence's threats, while not as bombastic as Trump's, had a degree of more power because of the cold and calm nature Pence spoke. His words were measured and filled with meaning in a way that only a man of integrity could speak.

Breaking Ties

The United States Constitution determines that the vice president is considered the *ex officio* president of the Senate. That entitles him to cast a vote in the Senate in the event of an even tie. To date, vice presidents have collectively case nearly 300 tie-breaking votes. Some vice presidents find themselves in the position of having to place a vote more often than others. Some, like Joe Biden and Dan Quayle, went through their entire terms without casting a single vote.

In Pence's case, he cast a total of 13 tie-breaking votes during his term. For example, in February 2017, he broke a tie in order to confirm Betsy DeVos as the secretary of education. Then, in March, he voted to advance a bill to defund Planned Parenthood.

In 2018, Pence made history by breaking a tie to confirm a judicial nominee, confirming Jonathan A. Kobes for the US Court of Appeals for the Eighth Circuit. At the time that Trump announced Kobes for the position, multiple organizations declared that he was not yet experienced enough with complex legal cases to be a circuit judge. Pence broke two ties with regard to Kobes' confirmation. First, there was the vote to invoke cloture on the nomination, a move that would force the debate over Kobes to come to a quick end. The invocation passed at 50-49 votes, with Pence breaking the tie. Then, about two weeks later, Pence once again cast a deciding tie-breaking vote, this time to confirm Kobes, who made it through on a 51-50 vote.

Kobes was the first federal judicial nominee to be confirmed by a tie-breaking vote, and it was Pence that pushed him over that line.

Another First For Pence

Pence also filed his own PAC (political action committee) in 2017. This made him the first-ever vice president to start such a committee while still in office. To put it in simple terms, a political action committee is an organization that pools campaign contributions and leverages them for political campaigns.

The PAC, called *Great America Committee*, was highly unusual, not just because it was filed by a sitting vice president. It was also unusual because the White House was under fire after the media reported on the Comey memos, a series of documents that James Comey led after his termination as Director of the FBI. The memos fueled the flames of controversy surrounding Russia's possible involvement in the 2016 presidential campaign. A special counsel was appointed to investigate Russian interference, and one day after that appointment, Pence filed the PAC.

Multiple news organizations found the timing of this filing awkward and concerning. Some even thought it meant Pence was jumping ship and starting early on a bid for the presidency in 2020. Pence called such allegation "laughable and absurd."

Still, this was a sure sign that things were heating up for the Trump-Pence campaign. While Trump was taking heat regarding Russia, a larger issue would appear in the form of Ukraine, and Pence would once again find himself walking a thin line between supporting his president and standing up for what he knew to be right.

Trump's Impeachment Inquiry

There are two independent issues behind the impeachment of Donald Trump. One has to do with asking a foreign party to investigate the family member of an American elected official. The second has to do with the concept of *quid pro quo*. Pence was key to the impeachment inquiry, but he chose to speak almost entirely on the first of those two issues, the issue that he had personal knowledge about.

To clarify, this was regarding Trump asking the President of Ukraine to investigate Hunter Biden, Joe Biden's son. This was because Hunter Biden was on a board in a Ukrainian country, receiving a hefty salary, at the same time that the US was providing a good deal of aid to the country—all while Joe Biden was serving as vice president.

Pence spoke on the phone with Volodymyr Zelensky, the President of Ukraine, on at least two occasions, and he also met with Zelensky in 2019. When he spoke to Zelensky, this was just after an unexpected delay in US military aid to Ukraine. Pence made it very clear that no *quid pro quo* was mentioned. In fact, Pence didn't speak to Zelensky regarding any kind of investigation into Hunter Biden. Instead, he raised issues regarding corruption in Ukraine in general.

That said, Pence was not against Trump calling

for an investigation into Joe and Hunter Biden. He testified, "I think the American people have a right to know if the vice president of the United States or his family profited from his position. [...] My predecessor had a son who was paid $50,000 a month to be on a Ukrainian board at the time that Vice President Biden was leading the Obama administration's efforts in Ukraine, I think that is worth looking into."

Pence chose to stay on the moral high ground, pointing out that an investigation was necessary without slinging accusations directly.

Trump was indeed impeached, but no charges were leveraged against him, and he never had to leave the White House. It seemed that the administration had dodged a major bullet. But, at the start of 2020, a new emergency was on the horizon: the COVID-19 pandemic, which we'll talk about in the following chapter.

CHAPTER 7

Re-Election Campaign

T he year 2020 started with another victory with the assassination of Qasem Soleimani, an Iranian major general in the Islamic Revolutionary Guard Corps. He was taken out via drone at the Baghdad International Airport as he was on his way to meet the Iraqi Prime Minister Adil Abdul-Mahdi in Baghdad.

Some were quick to criticize this action, but Pence jumped to Trump's defense, called Soleimani an evil man responsible for the deaths of American citizens because he assisted al-Qaeda prior to 9-11, among other things. In a tweet, Pence said that Soleimani had "assisted in the clandestine travel to Afghanistan of 10 of the 12 terrorists who carried out the September 11 terrorist attacks." People said that what Pence tweeted was wrong, especially without substantial evidence. For one thing, there were 19 terrorists involved in the September 11 attacks. However, it was later clarified that Pence was talking about the 12 terrorists now known to have traveled through Afghanistan prior to the attack. Ten out of the twelve had been "assisted by Soleimani," according to Pence's aid.

However, this victory for American justice was short-lived because another threat was already spreading elsewhere on the globe, a threat that can't be bombed by a drone: pandemic.

Covid-19 Taskforce

By February, it was clear that COVID-19 would be a national medical emergency. Trump tasked Pence with taking point on the White House Coronavirus Task Force. As part of this, Pence needed to understand how the virus was spreading and how to combat that spread in the best way possible. In order to carry out this hefty responsibility, Pence needed to coordinate with the Centers for Disease Control and Prevention, the Department of Health and Human Services, the National Institutes of Health, and the Department of Homeland Security.

Dealing with this was not always easy. Pence made choices in order to encourage the American public, quell panic, and present a strong image that people would look up to while at the same time leading by example in how to deal with the pandemic in the safest possible way. Knowing when to wear a mask and when not to, for example, was a hard choice to make. On one occasion, he opted not to wear a mask and was later criticized for that decision. He later admitted that he should have worn a mask at the time.

Meanwhile, Pence worked hard to keep people's spirits up by highlighting positive signs, such as a slight reduction in COVID cases. Finally, in December, Pence received the vaccine on live TV, showing Americans that the vaccine was safe and effective.

Re-Election Campaign

During the heat of the pandemic, the Trump-Pence administration was also focused on re-election. While some suggested that Trump drop Pence as a running partner in order to improve his chances, Trump showed loyalty, saying that Pence would absolutely stay on the ticket. Meanwhile, earlier in the year, Joe Biden had on several occasions remarked that Pence was a "decent guy," even when he was criticized by Democrats for making such a positive comment about "the enemy."

In October of 2020, things were not looking good for the Trump-Pence re-election campaign. Pence had a debate against Kamala Harris, and one poll showed that 59% felt that Harris had won the debate while only 38% felt that Pence had.

In early November, it was already obvious that Joe Biden had won, and Pence found himself in an impossible situation. Trump was calling the election a fraud, saying Biden had stolen the election while Trump had actually won it. Pence kept his wording on the safer side, emphasizing the need for integrity in the vote.

Trump started putting increasing pressure on Pence to overturn the vote. Pence pursued every legal avenue he could to delay the decision, looking for any signs of fraud. In the end, Pence had to make a decision—would he follow Trump or simply do his job as vice president to the best of his ability? Pence determined that it was best for Democracy to reign. If there was indeed fraud, that would have to be determined by the courts, but by a few rogue politicians.

The January 6 Attack

While Pence was in the Capitol, making a final count of the votes, Trump stirred up the people, insisting that the election had been a fraud. The official counting of the vote is normally a boring ceremony that nobody cares about. After all, it has already been established at this time who had won the election. Pence was determined to carry out his duty that day on January 6, but rogue elements saw this as a last chance to overthrow the election. Armed individuals gathered near the capitol, many even chanting that Pence should be hanged.

Pence and many other senators came dangerously close to the rioters that day as they stormed the capitol. Pence was ushered to an underground location, but he refused to leave via motorcade when given the chance. Instead of fleeing, Pence approved the deployment of the National Guard, an act that normally should be done by the president.

Thankfully, the rioter were cleared, and Congress was able to resume the ceremony that same evening, and Pence officially declared Biden and Harris the winners of the election.

CONCLUSION

The events of January 6, as well as Trump's response to COVID, the impeachment, collusion with Russia, and other controversies, would continue to be hot topics of discussion for years after Trump and Pence left the White House. Pence has come out of all of it much cleaner than Trump, with minimal criticism. In fact, as more details have come to light regarding the January 6 attack, in particular, Pence is being seen more and more as a hero than as a co-conspirator. Pence has shown himself to live up to the values behind the Bronze Star given to his father all those decades ago in Korea, values that Pence has worked to uphold his entire life.

Mike Pence has remained busy after leaving office. He joined the Heritage Foundation as a distinguished visiting fellow. He joined another conservative organization called Young America's Foundation.

Pence also narrated a television miniseries all about Rush Limbaugh, entitled *Age of Rush*. Pence said he felt honored to be a part of this memorial to the right-wing radio host, especially because Limbaugh was a major inspiration for him when he began his radio and television shows years back.

Speaking Tour Post-White House

Pence has been a highly sought-after speaker for many conservative events since the end of his term. During that time, Pence has slowly been distancing himself from the accusations Trump continues to make regarding the election of Joe Biden being a fraud. While many continually try to cast doubt regarding the election, Pence has turned his attention elsewhere. He also began to separate himself from Trump in other ways.

Pence has endorsed multiple candidates, and they are often different from the Republican candidates that Trump endorses.

As Pence continues to speak on a variety of conservative topics, one thing becomes increasingly clear: Mike Pence stands for what he believes in. Allegedly, at one point, Trump called Pence and yelled at him, saying, "Are you going to be a patriot or are you going to be a pussy?" These words were meant to bully Pence, but he did not take the bait.

Mike Pence has repeatedly shown throughout his career that he is indeed a patriot. He stands up for the same values he was taught as a child at home. He echoes the sentiments of political heroes before him, like JFK or Ronald Reagan, and he has proven time and again that he will not be strong-armed into leaving his patriotism behind.